Get Paid Without Ever Leaving Your House:

An Insiders Look at Making Money Working From Home

- - Minute Help Career Series --

By Rebecca Robinson

Minute Help Press

© 2010 All Rights Reserved

www.minutehelpguides.com

Table of Contents

INTRODUCTION 4

AVOIDING SCAMS 5
   QUESTIONS TO ASK POTENTIAL EMPLOYERS 5

JOBS & TRAINING 9
   SELF-ASSESSMENT QUESTIONS 9
   EXAMPLES OF TELECOMMUTING JOBS 10
      Freelance Writing and Editing................................11
      Software Programming and Engineering....................11
      Medical Transcriptionist..12
      Customer Service Representatives...........................13
      Salesperson..14
      Virtual Assistant..14
      Helpdesk..15

FINDING WORK 17
   WHERE TO FIND TELECOMMUTING JOBS 17
      Job Boards..17
      Classifieds..18
      Freelance Sites..18
   APPLYING FOR TELECOMMUTING JOBS 19
      Your Résumé..20
      Your Cover Letter...24
      First Contact..25
      The Interview...26
      Interview Questions..27
      The Job Offer...29
      Freelancing..29
   TELECOMMUTING CITIES IN THE UNITED STATES 31
   WORLDWIDE TELECOMMUTING CITIES............................35
   CHOOSING WHERE TO LIVE 42

MANAGING YOUR TIME 44
   COMPUTER & PERIPHERALS 50
   CHAIR & DESK 50

OFFICE	51
FINANCIAL CONSIDERATIONS	52
Health Care	*53*
Other Insurance	*54*
Vacation	*54*
Taxes	*54*
Perks	*55*
TAKING THE FIRST STEP	55
Cold Turkey	*56*
Slow and Steady	*56*
PEP TALK	56
ABOUT MINUTE HELP	**58**

Introduction

What is a telecommuter? In basic terms, it is someone who accesses their work through a computer that is off-site from their employer. However, a telecommuter can also be someone who is contracted on a work-for-hire basis to work for another party, or it can be someone who works for themselves. The premise of telecommuting is that you don't go to work; your work comes to you – whether it's at your home office or another location.

If you are considering becoming a telecommuter, then this eBook will help you explore your options, as well as the challenges and benefits of telecommuting.

Avoiding Scams

The first challenge when deciding to become a telecommuter is to find a job that will let you work from home. Your initial step should be to have a discussion with your current employer, if telecommuting would work for the type of job that you do. Prepare a plan, and explain the benefits of telecommuting to your employer.

If your current job will not allow telecommuting, then you have to find one that will. However, extreme caution is warranted, as there are many unscrupulous people out there who simply want to get money out of you. So approach each potential job with eagle eyes, and if at any time you feel like the offer is less than genuine it is time to walk away.

One major red flag is any employer who wants you to pay a "fee" to work for them. No actual employer will charge you for a job, so it is likely that this is a scam. You can also Google the employer or job and see what others have said about it. Like with any job opportunity, a fair amount of research is needed to ensure it is right for you.

Questions to Ask Potential Employers

If you have questions about an employer, ask! Any potential employer should be enthusiastic about answering your questions, and should offer more than basic answers to increase your comfort level. "Yes", "No", "I don't know", or "I can't answer that" answers are another red flag. Here are a few questions to ask a potential telecommuting employer:

1. Could you describe your organizational structure?
    - A "real" company should have a clear organizational structure with well-defined departments.

2. How do employees communicate with one another to carry out their work?
    - Good telecommuting companies have established communication methods, such as online work boards and instant messaging software.

3. What are the day-to-day responsibilities of this job?
    - What will your job be? If they can't tell you, this is a red flag.

4. What skills or abilities are necessary for someone to succeed in this job?

- If they have offered this type of job before, then they will know what is needed.

5. How much opportunity is there to see the end result of my efforts?
- Some of us prefer to see what happens to our work after we send it in.

6. How and by whom will my performance be reviewed, how often, and on what criteria?
- No job is complete without some type of performance review to let you know how you are doing, and whether there is room for improvement.

7. How much guidance or assistance is made available to individual telecommuters?
- Avoid employers who expect you do work in the dark, without any assistance.

8. Does your company provide additional training?
- A good company will be devoted to keeping you, and improving your skills.

9. What opportunities for advancement are there? Is there a management program?

- Unless you want to do the same job for the rest of your life, you will want to find a company that will let you grow.

10. What is your company's management style and what type of employee will fit in well with it?

- The company you choose should suit you and how you work. It's no fun to constantly butt heads with managers when your styles don't match up. Whether you prefer to be left alone or told what to do, your employers should have a management style that you can both work with.

Hopefully, by asking questions and conducting research about a company you can ensure that you find a real and viable telecommuting job.

Jobs & Training

So what types of jobs can you find as a telecommuter? Pretty much any job that doesn't require direct (person to person) contact with people can be a telecommuting job. Before you start applying for jobs, consider conducting a short self-assessment of your skills, as well as the types of jobs you prefer and excel at.

Self-Assessment Questions

By completing the questions below honestly, you can get a good idea of what types of jobs you are suited for.

1. Do you like working individually, or as part of a team?

2. Would you prefer a job that puts you in contact with the public?

3. Do you want the opportunity to make work-related decisions?

4. Are jobs with tight deadlines of interest to you?

5. Are you interested in sales, marketing, or some other field?

6. Would you like the opportunity to be creative in your new job?

7. Are you able to pay close attention to detail?

8. Do you want to work according to your own schedule?

9. Do you need a lot of job security?

10. Do you wish to supervise others?

While there are many other questions you can ask yourself, this assessment will give you a basic idea of which job opportunities are right for you, and which ones are not. Once you start researching the jobs themselves you can decide whether further training is necessary before you start sending in applications.

Examples of Telecommuting Jobs

Here are a few types of telecommuting jobs, and what they entail. Salary, training, and job demand information available through The Bureau of Labor Statistics website (www.bls.gov) has been included where available.

Freelance Writing and Editing

As a freelance writer you can pick and choose jobs. Competition is fierce, but once you develop a loyal client base and a reputation as a quality provider you can find regular well-paying work.

- Pros: Set your own hours, significant job variety.

- Cons: May have no jobs at times, jobs can be small or low-paying.

- Suited For: Creative, detail-orientated people who like to express themselves.

- Education Required: Varies, although those with a Bachelor's Degree in English or Journalism will have a definite advantage.

Software Programming and Engineering

There is huge demand for qualified software engineers, programmers and designers across the globe, and in many cases programmers and engineers can find gainful, steady employment with telecommute-friendly major companies. The Bureau of Labor Statistics expects a growth of 34% for Computer Software Engineers from 2008-2018, which is one of the highest growth rates across all jobs. They also report that the average salary in 2008 for a computer engineer was $85,430.

- Pros: Fast-paced, challenging, and rewarding.

- Cons: Requires significant attention to detail and group effort.

- Suited For: People who like working on computers with tight deadlines.

- Education Required: Generally at least an Associate of Science Degree, Bachelor's Degree preferred.

Medical Transcriptionist

Also known as a Medical Records and Health Information Technician, these employees can work for hospitals, health centers, or organizations that manage medical records. Medical Transcriptionists "read" clients medical files in order to help organizations manage health information and test results. A sub-section of this group includes medical billing and coding, which involves assigning codes to procedures so health insurance companies can be billed. From 2008-2010 it is expected that this field will grow by 20%, and the average salary in 2008 was $30,610.

- Pros: Lots of work, make your own hours.

- Cons: Repetitive, detail-oriented.

- Suited For: Someone who wants steady work, with little variation or interaction.

- Education Required: Usually a one to two-year program designed at teaching students the ins and outs of transcribing and the programs used. Most programs are available online.

Customer Service Representatives

Considered one of the largest single occupations in the United States, Customer Service Representatives can be found at nearly every type of company. Many companies are contracting out their customer services to call centers, which in turn opens up telecommuting opportunities. The average pay for a customer service representative is $14.36 per hour, and this field is expected to grow 18% through 2018.

- Pros: Interact with the public and help people.

- Cons: May need to deal with difficult people, set hours, pay is average.

- Suited For: People who like to help other people.

- Education Required: Opportunities exist for all levels, but those with a background in customer service will have the advantage.

Salesperson

People who are good with other people are often very good in sales, which is another area where there are telecommuting jobs. In general these jobs involve selling goods or services over the phone, either by "cold calling" potential customers or being provided a list. Expected to grow 8% from 2008-2018, Salespeople can expect to earn about $10 per hour, including commissions.

- Pros: The better you are, the more you earn.

- Cons: Not suited for everyone, must be able to interact well with people.

- Suited For: Friendly, sociable types.

- Education Required: Minimal.

Virtual Assistant

Instead of working in an office to help an executive, virtual assistants work from their own home. They may send e-mails and faxes, make phone calls and appointments, make travel arrangements and put together reports. Overall, the Administrative Assistant and Secretary field is expected to grow by 11% from 2008-2018, but many companies are choosing Virtual Assistants to save on employee costs. Administrative Assistants and Secretaries earned $29,050 in 2008.

- Pros: No boss over your shoulder.

- Cons: Have to be ready to help during employer's work hours.

- Suited For: Stay at home parents who are comfortable using computers.

- Education Required: Must have computer experience, a few courses in bookkeeping, desktop publishing, etc. will provide an advantage.

Helpdesk

Those who enjoy solving problems and using computers are well suited for helpdesk work. Like customer service, nearly every company has a helpdesk department to assist customers in using a product, tracking a shipment, or finding a solution. Customer Support Specialists are the most advanced workers in this field, and earned an average of $43,450 in 2008.

- Pros: Help people solve problems.

- Cons: Occasional difficult clients, may need to work nights or weekends.

- Suited For: Computer people who like to interact with the public.

- Education Required: Some companies may provide training, Computer Support

Specialists will have an advantage if they have completed an Associate of Science Degree.

The next step, once you have decided on the type of telecommuting job you are suited for, is to find jobs and send in your application!

"Work is love made visible. And if you cannot work with love but only with distaste, it is better that you should leave your work and sit at the gate of the temple and take alms of those who work with joy." ~ Kahlil Gibran

Finding Work

So where are all these great telecommuting jobs? And how do you apply for, and get them? Take it easy, we'll break it down for you.

Where to Find Telecommuting Jobs

Job Boards
The first place to start is major job boards. While you may have to dig for a bit to find any good jobs, if you have the types of positions you are interested in it should be easy to search. Note that not all job postings will say "telecommuting" or "work from home," so you may have to do some digging.

Here are a few job boards to check out:

- Monster.com
- Hotjobs.com
- Job-Hunt.org
- Flexjobs.com

Classifieds

Because a telecommuting job is not your "ordinary" job, you may have to look in non-ordinary places for these opportunities. Classified ad websites that have a help wanted section are another good place to look. Here are some examples:

- Craigslist.org
- Cavegoat.com
- USNetAds.com

Free classified ads online should be approached carefully, since there is little done in the way of verifying the poster. Do not give out personal information – such as your address or social security number – until you are sure that you are dealing with a real company.

Freelance Sites

If you like the idea of working for yourself, then there are many sites out there for freelancers. Basically you are a provider, and you have clients instead of employers. Jobs can run for one day or several months, so you have to be comfortable with the ebb and flow. Some good freelance sites include:

- Elance.com
- Freelancewritinggigs.com

- Freelancer.com
- Odesk.com

Note that most of these sites have some type of remuneration system; they may charge you to bid on jobs, have a monthly membership system, or charge a commission on jobs that you obtain through the site. The benefit of these types of sites is that they usually have a payment system which ensures that you get paid when you complete your work, so you don't have to worry about someone running off without paying.

Applying for Telecommuting Jobs

Just like any job, applying for a telecommuting job takes some finesse and patience. Above all, make sure that you follow the job proposal procedure outlined in the job posting; otherwise you might as well not apply at all.

Your Résumé

No matter what type of job you are applying for, you need a good résumé to sell yourself. A good résumé should tell people why they should hire you, and should be to the point. Remember that employers may have to go through many résumés, and will likely not spend more than 30 seconds looking at yours. So make it count.

Have someone else look over your résumé, whether it is a friend or a professional. There should be no spelling mistakes or grammatical errors, and it should be neatly laid out. You may have to create several versions of your résumé, as it is good to tailor your résumé to suit the requirements of different employers (this doesn't mean fabricating details, it just means highlighting the points they are interested in and leaving out those they don't care about).

The basic elements of a good résumé are as follows:

Title

> Your résumé begins with your full name, in bold and centered at the top of the page. The font should be larger than the rest of the text. While most résumés include your address after your name on a new line, due to the anonymity of online jobs you may just want to include your city and state. Also include your phone number and e-mail address.

Career Summary

This section is commonly used by older, more experienced applicants, and can state your experiences for the last few years in one paragraph.

Career Objective

For less experienced applicants, this section is a statement of "where you want to go". State what your ideal career objective is for the immediate future, and how your existing experience applies. Ensure that your career objective is in line with the job you are applying for.

Experience

This is essentially your work history, and should only appear before the Education/Training section if you have significant experience. Your history is listed chronologically, starting with the most recent. Information to list includes:

- Name of Company
- Job Title
- Time Worked (ie: January 2008 – October 2010)

- Responsibilities
- Special Achievements (ie: Top Salesman 2009, Employee of the Year, etc.)

Ideally, short-term jobs should not be mentioned unless leaving them out would result in a significant gap in your work history.

Education / Training

This section comes before Experience if you are new to the job market (like a recent graduate). Information to include:

- Name of Degree
- Institution Name
- Years attended
- Achievements (ie: Graduate Summa Cum Laude, Valedictorian, etc.)

You can indicate that a degree is "ongoing" if you have not completed it. Also include any training that you may have completed that is directly relevant to the job you are applying for. You can put related internship work in the Experience or Additional Information category.

Additional Information

This is a great place to include other information that makes you a good candidate for the job you are applying for. Examples include:

- Professional Achievements & Awards
- Languages
- Specific Computer Skills
- Licenses
- Volunteer Work

Personal Information

If you wish you can include a short biography, or mention what you like to do in your spare time.

References

Generally, including "references available upon request" is sufficient if you are not comfortable giving out reference information during the initial application. Two to three references is the norm, and your information should include their name and contact information, as well as a sentence describing how they know you. You should never list a relative as a reference.

Your Cover Letter

A cover letter is an excellent way to set yourself apart from the crowd. In many job postings it may be a necessity, so make sure you read it carefully. Your cover letter should be written like a regular letter, addressed to the company or job contact. Your letter should begin by stating the job you are applying for, and where you found it.

The bulk of your letter should indicate why the job is suited for you. Link previous experiences, education, or training to the job posting so the hirer gets a good idea of whether you will fit with the company. The cover letter should be clear, precise, and to the point.

The close of the letter should indicate your availability, and whether you have attached any other information (like your résumé). Thank the reader for their time and consideration, and close the letter with "Sincerely, Your Name". If you need help writing your cover letter, ask an employed friend, or search for cover letter on the Internet. There are lots of resources available.

Remember that your cover letter should be specific for the job you are applying for, so you may have to revise it every time you apply for a job. While this is time-consuming, a good cover letter can make the difference between the trash can and a phone call.

First Contact

Generally, when you submit your résumé for a job via a job board, website, or e-mail you will receive a standard "Thank you for your interest…" response. If the employer is interested in your abilities and experience they may short-list you for initial contact, which can be an e-mail, online chat, or phone call.

When you are talking to the employer, always be professional. While that may be difficult in an electronic communication environment, it is very important. This means no smiley faces or text-speak (LOL, BTW, etc.) Before you send an e-mail or instant message, proofread your response. The last thing you want is to get crossed off the list due to a spelling mistake.

Hopefully, if initial contact goes well and you are still a good candidate for the job you will be invited for an interview.

The Interview

If you think that you may be contacted for an interview make sure you are prepared. For one, if you have provided them with a phone number you need to be available. No one likes to play phone tag, so carry your cell phone and keep it charged. Here are some other things to have on hand:

- A copy of your résumé
- A pen and paper to take notes
- A list of accomplishments
- A list of questions you would like to ask
- A glass of water

During the interview you will want to listen carefully to the questions, take a moment to formulate a response, and answer clearly. Refer to the person by "Mr." or "Mrs." unless they ask you specifically to call them by their first name. Smile! This sounds weird since they can't see you, but it does affect your tone of voice and makes it sound more positive and friendly. Keep your answers short and to the point. At the end of the interview remember to thank them.

After the interview you may want to write down your thoughts and any questions you may have. Send the interviewer a quick e-mail thanking them for calling, and reiterate your interest in the job.

Interview Questions

It's best to be prepared for an interview, so you can give great answers. Here are some common interview questions:

Job History

- Name of previous employer, job title, description, dates (have résumé handy)
- Salary at start and end of job
- Responsibilities
- Major challenges and outcomes
- Reason for leaving

New Job

- What is it that interests you about this job?
- What education or experience makes you the best candidate?
- Are you overqualified for this job?
- Why do you want to work for us?
- What do you bring to the table?

Personal Questions

- What is important to you in a job?
- What is your greatest strength / weakness?
- How do you handle stress?
- What motivates you?
- What is your typical work week?
- What are your career goals?

Like most things in life there are very few wrong answers, but you still want to try to have the best answer. Spend some time answering these questions to yourself, and see how it sounds. If you are unsure about your interview skills have a mock phone interview with a friend. Sometimes recording your interview can give you good hints about where you need improvement. Remember there are tons of websites out there devoted to the "best" answer, so head online if you need more help.

After your initial interview, you may have to have one or two more interviews – particularly if there is a large pool of candidates. Be patient and keep smiling!

The Job Offer

Eventually, after much hard work and determination you will get a job offer. Congrats! Before you sign the dotted line, review your options carefully. What does the offer include? Is the salary sufficient, or is there at least an opportunity to earn more? Will they pay for training and equipment if necessary? Make sure you are 100% comfortable with the terms of employment before you commit to anything.

Freelancing

If you are choosing the freelance route, then your journey to gainful employment will be slightly different. In general a freelance job goes like this:

- You find a job posting and submit your Request For Proposal (RFP)

- Your RFP can include a résumé, but also includes all the terms of the job, and your price (per hour, page, project, etc.)

- You have some back and forth with the client via e-mail, text, or phone

- Your offer is accepted and you start work

- You get paid as per the terms of your RFP

While freelancing offers much more freedom in who you work for, it also has less job security – as you are only "employed" for as long as the proposal states, and then the cycle starts over again. You may have one client or several at the same time, and may have to juggle multiple deadlines. It's up to you as to which avenue you want to pursue. You can always try one route and then switch to the other if it doesn't work out the way you planned.

"Don't be afraid to give your best to what seemingly are small jobs. Every time you conquer one it makes you that much stronger. If you do the little jobs well, the big ones will tend to take care of themselves." ~
Dale Carnegie

Best Places to Live

One of the primary reasons to telecommute is that you can work anywhere – literally. As long as you have access to the technology you need to stay connected and get your job done you can move wherever you like. So where should you go? Here are some of the top telecommuting cities:

Telecommuting Cities in the United States

Sometimes we just like what is familiar, so we stick close to home. If where you live now is too expensive, or if you are having difficulty pinpointing telecommuting jobs in the area, then you may want to consider moving to one of these great telecommuting cities:

1. Washington, D.C.: This has been named the top telecommuting city by *Sperling's Best Places* as well as Intel Computers due to its high number of white collar jobs and the cost of commuting. Now that the government is getting on board with telecommuting you can certainly find good work from home jobs here at local companies. It's also a great place to get in touch with American History.

2. Boston, M.A.: Both *Sperling's Best Places* and Microsoft name this city one of the best,

due to the high level of support provided by companies who are encouraging telecommuting. Those who want to upgrade their technical skills can also easily access programs at MIT.

3. Edeb Prarie, M.N.: Never heard of it? This small town of just 64,000 residents was voted the best place to live in 2010 by CNN for its strong economy and natural beauty. It's has very affordable housing and a great community.

4. San Francisco, C.A.: Since it costs so much to own a car in this city, and the high number of computer-related jobs here, it's easy to see why this city ranks so high. While the cost of living is fairly high, finding affordable housing just outside of the city is not a problem, and you'll still get a chance to ride on the trolley cars.

5. Raleigh-Durham, N.C.: A great place to raise kids, this smaller city has excellent Internet connectivity and lots of Universities for those who want to increase their skill levels.

6. Seattle, W.A.: The tech-heavy city of Seattle may have lots of rain, but it is an outdoor person's paradise, and has a lower cost of living than some of the other geek-friendly

cities. There are also many high-tech schools in the area for those who need an upgrade.

7. Austin, T.X.: This developing city has a lot to offer, including many major computer, health care and technological firms. Finding affordable housing is not a problem, and there are a ton of activities to occupy your off-time.

8. Phoenix, A.Z.: Those who love sun year-round will enjoy Phoenix. There are many opportunities for outdoor activities, so you can enjoy your new found freedom when you take a break from working.

9. Syracuse, N.Y.: Considered an inexpensive place to live, you can get a home here for amazingly cheap, but still be close to the action of the Big Apple, as well as the influx of telecommuting jobs.

10. Anchorage, A.K.: While it's cold and doesn't get a lot of sun in the winter, this is a peaceful place for those who need to get away from it all, and it is incredibly inexpensive to live here. Grab a parka and see what it's all about.

11. Atlanta, G.A.: Offers a great blend of good Internet connectivity and lower than average cost of living. It also has great weather and is within driving distance of the beautiful Eastern coastline if you are up for a road trip.

12. Santa Fe, New Mexico: With the jump on green technology, this city is terrific place to call home and find work, and has a low cost of living. There are tons of parks to explore, and you can head across the border for a vacation when you need it.

13. Salt Lake City, U.T.: Has been frequently voted one of the best places to find work, and has a large base of technology employers to choose from. Also offers a wide variety of outdoor recreational activities.

14. Colorado Springs, C.O.: If you love being outdoors then Colorado Springs is the place to be. It has been ranked the fittest city in the United States and offers year-round opportunities for enjoying nature.

15. New York City, N.Y.: Sure the cost of living is high, but if you're telecommuting you can easily live in the suburbs and still be close to all the action and entertainment this city has to offer. There are some great tech schools here too.

16. Chicago, I.L.: A great place to visit, and also to live. Chicago is a bustling metropolis, full of job opportunities and entertainment.

17. Miami, F.L.: Warm, sub-tropical, and sunny – what else do you need? It is surprisingly

affordable to live in Miami, and offers a unique culture not found anywhere else in the U.S.

18. Honolulu, H.I.: Here's another warm place to call home. Go surfing, diving, sailing, or whatever you want – just remember to get back to work once in a while. While the cost of living is a bit high, the benefits are endless.

19. Bellevue, W.A.: Forests surround this lovely city, which although small is now home to major players like Microsoft and Verizon. Houses here are affordable, and Seattle is close by for those who need the entertainment scene, or want to continue their education.

20. Columbia, M.D.: Also called Ellicott City, this town of 155,000 residents has a ton of parkland and is home to major music festivals. It also boasts a low jobless rate, and is close to Baltimore and D.C. for those who need to stay in contact with the big cities. It also is home to a very low foreclosure rate and affordable homes.

Worldwide Telecommuting Cities

If you're not going to be in an office anyway, why not take your telecommuting somewhere more exotic? There are a ton of great cities throughout the world that offer a combination of reasonable costs of living, good job opportunities, and great internet service, such as:

1. Vancouver, Canada: This "green" city has everything – night life, world-class skiing, entertainment, as well as a plethora of telecommuting opportunities and recognized Universities.

2. Copenhagen, Denmark: Who can dispute one of the happiest cities in the world? As a bonus this is one of the lowest costing cities to live.

3. Seoul, South Korea: Considered one of the most Internet-friendly places to live, if you feel the need to go abroad with broadband then this is it. They also have a significant technological presence, so you can look for local telecommuting jobs while you are there.

4. Taipei, Taiwan: This city was on the forefront of the telecommuting trend, and offers a ton of opportunities for those with entrepreneurial spirit.

5. Auckland, New Zealand: Located on the North Island of the country, Auckland is home to over 1.4 million residents. Rated fourth in

the world by Mercer, this city offers a relaxed atmosphere and has one of the highest home ownership rates in the world.

6. Cordoba, Argentina: An amazing South American city that is rich in culture, Cordoba has everything you need to stay wired and connect with history, and is very affordable.

7. Barcelona, Spain: Barcelona is considered the best place for singles, so if you're single and looking for some romance then you may want to head here. It is also a good place for creative minds who like good food.

8. Bangalore, India: Beautiful and inexpensive, there are wireless cafes all over the city – so you don't have to stay home to work. This is also one of largest sources of outsourced workers in the world – so it's a good place to find telecommuting opportunities.

9. Mexico City, Mexico: A big city with lots of opportunities, you can find a great telecommuting job, live cheaply, and still be able to visit friends and family State-side easily.

10. Stockholm, Sweden: For coders and developers, Stockholm is the birthplace of open source code. It is also a beautiful city

with tons of history, and regularly ranks at the top for the best place to live in the world.

11. Munich, Germany: Voted 7th in the world by Mercer, this city is a major financial hub for British ex-patriots, and home to many major financial centers. It is also the perfect place to explore the history of the country, and to drink great beer.

12. Melbourne, Australia: This city has so much to offer for nature lovers and urbanites alike. Beaches abound, as do funky shops. In fact you may have a hard time remembering to work while you live here.

13. Singapore: This island Mecca is a hub for technological companies, making it an easy place to find telecommuting work. With an extremely low crime rate, you'll also feel safe and enjoy a high standard of living.

14. Prague, Czech Republic: Rich in history and with a lower cost of living than other European cities, this is the place to go if you love architecture. As a plus it is easy to travel to Germany and Austria for weekend adventures.

15. Dubai, UAE: This city has the highest quality of living in the entire Middle East, and is also considered the fastest growing city in the

world. Opportunities abound for telecommuters here, as it is home to many high-tech companies.

16. Buenos Aires, Argentina: Full of history and culture, this is the place to go if you love art. It also has a relatively low cost of living, and is a beautiful place to live.

17. Vienna, Austria: This capital city has a nice even climate and amazing history, as well as plenty of museums to explore. Plus you can get good coffee, which is a must when you are working overtime on your latest project.

18. Zurich, Switzerland: Home to some of the world's largest financial centers, this is a good place to find steady employment while enjoying some amazing scenery.

19. Sydney, Australia: Considered one of the largest multicultural cities in the world, Sydney has everything you want, including affordable housing and great telecommuting opportunities.

20. Brussels, Belgium: With more than 80 museums, Brussels is an art lover's paradise and a fantastic place to live. Come for the culture, stay for the chocolate!

21. Geneva, Switzerland: Considered the third-largest financial center in Europe, Geneva is home to many large banks and financial companies, which means many opportunities for telecommuters. However, it is also the fourth most expensive city in the world, so be prepared to work hard.

22. Frankfurt, Germany: This fifth-largest German city is home to over 600,000 people, and is the financial epicenter of the country. Offering festivals, museums, incredible food, and dance music, you'll never run out of things to see and do. As an added plus the housing market is quite stable here.

23. Amsterdam, Netherlands: If you prefer more of a relaxed, alternative lifestyle then Amsterdam is the place for you. It is also home to exceptional art exhibits, and has a ton of culture. While living in Amsterdam isn't cheap, you won't need a car since the public transportation system is exceptional.

24. Ottawa, Canada: The capital of this country is home to some major companies, and the outlying suburbs provide a quiet and relaxed lifestyle. Once you get used to the cold winters you'll love being able to go ice fishing, skiing, and snowmobiling whenever you like. Mercer has rated Ottawa the 3rd

cleanest city in the world – now that's something!

25. Luxembourg, Grand Duchy or Luxembourg: This tiny country has over a half million residents, and is ruled by a Grand Duke. Located next to France, Germany, and Belgium it is the perfect place for telecommuters who want to immerse themselves in a true European culture. The country boasts a great economy with low inflation and unemployment.

26. Perth, Australia: This capital of Western Australia is truly a stunning blend of city and nature. There are many major companies based here, and recently there has been a shift toward service-orientated industries. Perth has also been dubbed the "new Seattle" for their emerging music culture.

27. Oslo, Norway: This hub of Norwegian trade is a prime location for the maritime industry and is home to some of the world's largest shipping companies. It is also the world's most expensive city, so those who choose to move here need to be ready to work hard.

28. Dublin, Ireland: With the phenomenal economic growth this city has seen over the last 10 years, it is no wonder that Dublin has become one of the top places to live in the

world. Offering the second highest wages in the world, this is the place to go to earn money and enjoy local fare.

29. Hamburg, Germany: Home to 1.8 million people, the port of Hamburg is the major economic force in this country, and has helped it become one of the most affluent cities in Europe. There is also a significant aerospace presence, and many media businesses looking for good workers.

30. Paris, France: Who could forget Paris? Romantic, beautiful, and fun, this city has it all. However, it is also considered one of the most expensive places to live. Luckily you can survive without a car in Paris, and you can save by renting outside the city.

Choosing Where to Live

Before you pull up roots and head out into a new adventure, you'll need to do some research on your new location. Here are some points to investigate:

- Availability of high speed /wireless internet
- Cost of housing
- Availability of rentals / housing

- Cost of basic necessities (food, clothing, internet service)
- Crime rate

Since you will be telecommuting, job opportunities in the city you are moving to aren't of the highest importance. However, many companies may prefer to give telecommuting opportunities to those who are nearby, so this can be a consideration.

Finally, when you've chosen your destination it's a good idea to visit before you make any final plans. Check out the city, find the areas where you would prefer to live, and make a few local connections for housing. Plan to stay for at least a few days, or as much time as you'll need to get a feel for the city.

Remember that the city you choose does not have to be your "final destination" – as a telecommuter you can always pack up and move on. So if you've always wanted to live in Paris or another high-cost city, why not give it a try? After a few months or years you can balance out your expenses by moving somewhere more affordable. The opportunities are endless.

"Living on Earth may be expensive, but it includes an annual free trip around the Sun." ~ Unknown

Managing your Time

The biggest challenge that telecommuters face is managing their time. Since they are in charge of their schedule, when they work, and how hard they work it can be difficult to focus. Here are some tips on managing time:

Make a Schedule

Just like a standard job, you need to have a work schedule – and you need to stick to it. If you find that non-work items need to be attended to (particularly with children around) then it is good to schedule your work in 1-2 hour blocks, so you can break in between and deal with what needs to be taken care of.

You can also choose to work when your family is at work, school, or asleep. The important thing is that you have enough time to work, during the hours you prefer to work, and that you can get work completed during those hours.

Avoid Distractions

Anything that distracts you from work will cut into your productivity, so it is important that you stay focused. That means non-work related distractions need to be avoided whenever possible. In this vein, it is a good idea to have a work e-mail, so you don't get side-tracked by personal communications.

Also avoid any online activities that are not work-related – such as Facebook. During your break feel free to browse, but when it is work time try to stay focused. It will result in higher productivity and less time spent working if you can shut down distractions as much as possible.

Turn it Off

The problem with working from home is that your work is always there waiting for you, so it's hard to turn it off when you're not supposed to be working. However, it also isn't fair to your family if you are checking e-mails when you're supposed to be spending quality time.

If you need to stay in regular contact with employers or clients, then set these times aside as work time, and try to keep it as the same time each day. The rest of the time you are not on the clock, so stay away from your computer! By clearly defining your work and non-work time you will find it easier to "let go" and focus on being with your family.

Stay Organized

Managing your jobs and deadlines is important, because if you don't you may find that you are either stressed from over-work, or out of a job. Keep clear track of when jobs need to be completed, and the milestones that need to be completed within each job.

If it helps, there are many online programs and downloadable software that can help you stay organized. For others, a plain-paper planner or organizer may be more helpful. Whichever way works, as long as it helps you stay on track.

Stay Connected

One of the downfalls of telecommuting is you don't get that daily interaction with other people, which can lead to feeling cut-off from the rest of the world. This can lead to depression, anxiety, and resentment towards other family members.

Make it a point to get out of the house once in a while. Once or twice a week try to find a group activity that you can do outside of work – like yoga or aerobics. Don't neglect your friends (outside of work hours), and remember that the primary advantage of working from home is that you are supposed to have more time to do non-work activities.

It can also be a good idea to build a network of online professionals that you can connect with. They can help when you get stuck on a project, or listen when you need to vent. There are quite a few online forums and communities for freelancers and telecommuters, like the following:

http://www.work-at-home-forum.com/

http://www.whydowork.com/

http://www.honestworkfromhomesuccess.com/work-home-community/

http://www.elance.com/p/community/talk/index.html

Do Mundane Tasks First

The hardest part about managing your time is finding the time (and energy) to do those mundane tasks. After all, it is so much more fun to tackle new projects then to tidy up the odds and ends of old ones. However, unless you want to find yourself stuck with a ton of work – both fun and not fun – it's a good idea to get those odds and ends out of the way.

Set aside an hour (or however much time you need) per week to get caught up on your loose ends so they don't pile up on you. Make it the same time each week, and don't procrastinate.

When Delays Occur

It is inevitable, in both the telecommuting world and at traditional jobs that delays and interruptions will occur. Kids get sick, cars get into accidents, and family emergencies pop up when you can least prepare for them. However, you will find that in a telecommuting environment your employer or clients are less understanding when your project is delayed, no matter what the reason. How you handle the delay and follow up will have a large impact on whether your career with that particular employer or client continues. Here are some suggestions:

- *Inform ASAP*: Let them know as soon as you can about the delay, so if they have to make arrangements on their end they can.

- *Be Honest*: If you have suffered a major loss or have to travel a fair distance, make sure they know that you may not be "back" to work for some time. Don't lie, and don't sugar coat.

- *Give Updates*: Employers get nervous when a staff member disappears from their team, so send updates every few days to let them know you are still on the team, but just on a temporary hiatus.

- *Offer Alternatives*: If you have a friend or colleague who can fill your shoes while you are off, then let them know. Not everyone will be up to taking on another team member, but for some time-sensitive projects they may appreciate that you have thought of how to help.

- *Get Back ASAP*: While some issues take longer to resolve than others, it is important that you return to work as soon as you are able. Remember that others are counting on you, and as your primary source of revenue you can't afford to stay off work for too long.

By minimizing delays you not only ensure that your client or employer can keep the project going, it can also help ensure that you have a job to come back to. It can be good to have an emergency plan in place, just in case you need it.

> **"Work joyfully and peacefully, knowing that right thoughts and right efforts will inevitably bring about right results."** ~ *James Allen*

Setting up a home office

In order to telecommute, you need a home office. For some, it may be as simple as a wireless laptop, while others may need more complicated equipment. It all depends on the job, your budget, and what you personally need to work comfortably.

Computer & Peripherals

No matter what type of telecommuter you are, you need a good computer. It needs to be reliable and have the ability to run efficiently. In general it is a good idea to have a separate computer for work, so your kids or spouse doesn't wreck it with viruses and bloated programs, or bug you to use it while you need to concentrate on work.

A laptop is great if you like mobility, but may not be as comfortable to work on as a personal computer. Laptops are usually a bit more expensive than a similarly equipped home computer, so factor this into your budget.

Other items may include

- Web Camera
- Microphone or Headset
- Mouse and Keyboard
- Printer / Fax / Scanner

Chair & Desk

While it may not seem important now, these are the two most important items in your office. Your chair must be comfortable and adjustable if possible. If you buy a cheap chair and are not comfortable you will find that your work suffers, and that you don't enjoy going to work in the morning. Since you are a business operator, you can usually write off these expenses at the end of the year, so invest in yourself by getting the equipment that will help you be productive.

Your desk should be large enough to fit what you need, but not feel oppressive or take up the whole room. Some people like to have shelves, so they can see the items they need easily, while others like drawers to keep items cleared away. Go to an office furniture store and see what you like. If you are on a tight budget then try the classifieds or a second-hand store.

Office

Ideally your office is in a quiet location in your home, so you don't get distracted by family members when you are working. Not everyone has a home that is large enough for its own office, so a quiet corner in a basement or family room may be the best you can manage for now. It's not a good idea to set up an office in your bedroom, as you may find that it is difficult to not think about work while you are in bed, since your work is sitting in the room with you.

Your workspace should be comfortable and well lit. Buy a lamp or two to light up the space, hang a few pictures or posters, and buy a small heater or fan to keep the temperature where you like it. The more at home you feel at work (even when it's at home) the more productive you can be.

Other Tips

Financial Considerations

Now that you know the ins and outs of telecommuting, you will likely want to sit down and figure out your finances to see if you can make it work. A good starting point is your savings – can it support you while you search for telecommuting work? It is recommended to have about 6 months of expenses saved up before you start looking, so you don't end up in financial straits. The last thing you want is to have to remortgage your house or worse.

However, your savings and finances are not the only aspects to think about. There are other expenses and factors to consider before you make your final decision about telecommuting.

Health Care

Most companies hire their telecommuters as independent contractors, which results in no company health insurance. Can you afford to pay for health insurance coverage out of pocket? If your spouse has coverage this may be a non-issue, but make sure you figure this out first. Shop around and find an insurance policy that provides good coverage, but doesn't cost an arm and a leg.

Other Insurance

There are other insurance factors to think about before you start telecommuting. What if you hurt yourself or become ill and cannot work? What if a family member becomes ill and you need to care for them? There is always disability and other types of insurance that can help, but you need to budget for the costs of the policy.

Vacation

Depending on whom you work for and the arrangements, you may no longer be entitled to vacation pay or time off. You will have to budget for vacations, and balance your work load carefully so you can take time off when you decide to go away. You also may have difficulty committing to work when your kids are home for Christmas or Spring Break, so your budget will have to account for child care or camps, or time off during these periods.

Taxes

As an independent contractor or freelancer you will be paid in full, with no deductions for taxes. It is recommended that you make regular payments to the IRS throughout the year, so you don't have to pay huge penalties at the end of the year.

The taxes that you owe on the income you make is based on your net income after expenses; this means anything you buy for the business (office supplies, Internet, cell phone bills, office rent, etc.) should be deducted, and then you take out the percentage for the IRS.

Each state varies with regards to how you will be taxed. The Federal government, however, always stays the same. If you file as a single person, then any income you have above $34,000 but below $82,400 is subject to federal taxes (25%), plus social security and Medicare taxes (another 15.3%). So about 40% of your income should be taken out and sent quarterly to the Federal (plus whatever your state requires).

To submit an estimated tax payment, you will need to fill out Form 1040-ES (Estimated Tax for Individuals), which can be downloaded online at www.irs.gov. It is submitted quarterly (check the dates on the form to ensure that you get it in on time, as they change yearly); payment can be made either by check or electronically.

Perks

You can say goodbye to those company perks you were so fond of as well. If you are getting a discount on a gym membership, hotel stays, or anything else through work you likely will have to give them up for good, or budget for the difference.

Taking the First Step

Once you have decided that telecommuting is for you, how do you get started? There are really two ways to go about it. Which one you choose depends entirely on your comfort level.

Cold Turkey

In this scenario you quit your day job and start concentrating on finding telecommuting work immediately. While you will be able to focus wholly on creating a perfect résumé and applying for jobs, this route also puts significant financial strain on you and your family. This option is great if you have savings you can count on or if your current job takes up so much time and energy that you'd never find the time to look for work otherwise.

Slow and Steady

If you have some free time already, or are able to cut your work hours back, then you can "ease in" to telecommuting, perhaps with a regular part-time job or a few freelancing gigs. This method lets you get a feel for telecommuting, without burning your bridges at your current job in case things don't work out. It also gives you a financial safety net in case your savings are not enough to get by, or if you are not sure whether you can earn enough telecommuting.

Pep Talk

There will be times when you are making the transition to telecommuting when you get frustrated and just want to give up. Don't! Telecommuting is a business unto itself, and like any business it takes a lot of hard work and determination before you will see results. Find a forum to talk about your fears and frustrations, or take a few classes to build up your skills. If you are good at what you do, then there is no reason why you shouldn't be able to be a successful telecommuter.

> *"Find something you love to do and you'll never have to work a day in your life"* ~ *Harvey MacKay*

About Minute Help

Minute Help Press is building a library of books for people with only minutes to spare. Follow @minutehelp on Twitter to receive the latest information about free and paid publications from Minute Help Press, or visit minutehelpguides.com.

www.ingramcontent.com/pod-product-compliance
Lightning Source LLC
Chambersburg PA
CBHW072048190526
45165CB00019B/2188